R - RETURN TO EDEN

BOOK 1 IN THE "REMAIN" SERIES

DART EASTWOOD

CONTENTS

INTRODUCTION

In John 15:4-5 Jesus tells us, "Remain in Me, and I in you. Just as the branch cannot bear fruit of itself but must remain in the vine, so neither can you unless you remain in Me. I am the vine, you are the branches; the one who remains in Me, and I in him bears much fruit, for apart from Me you can do nothing."

This REMAIN series seeks to help us deepen our relationship and walk with Jesus. Dart's transparency in these books helps guide and encourage us to focus on following God, seeking His will, and trusting His love for us so we can in turn love ourselves and love others. Each book has its own focus...

R - Return to Eden... It's NOT about religion, but it's ALL about relationship. There was no religion in the garden. It was a relationship with God. He would come and walk with them in the cool of the day. (Genesis 3:8) This first collection in the REMAIN series gracefully dives into our relationship with God... and His relationship with us.

FOLLOW ME

FOLLOWING IS AN ACTION

*M*ost of us read the Bible, but have no idea how it applies to our lives. Especially RIGHT NOW in the situation we're dealing with.

This.

Very.

Moment.

We read it and the stories are from a different time and a different place. The culture is different. The laws are different. How does any of this apply to MY life? How does this help ME?

Now, let me be clear... the Bible is the most amazing book ever. It's not only a love letter written to us, (yes, TO us, as well as FOR us,) but it's also a roadmap of how to navigate this world. It may not have directions for your specific location right this instant, but the stories and directions and guidance given throughout does give you general guidelines for where to turn.

But... HOW do we apply it to our lives??

The Bible was never meant to have ALL the answers for us, for each specific thing we are going through this very instant. Remember, this wasn't how things started. Adam and Eve didn't have the Bible. They had a relationship with God. That's how this was all designed. That was the intention from the beginning... for us to be in a relationship WITH Him, not in a religion FOR Him.

Of course, we all know what happens. We decide we know best and we go our own way. When that relationship was broken by sin and we (humans) no longer spoke with God every day, He had people start writing things down for us, giving us rules and guidelines and directions on how to live our lives. He gave us stories and examples of what happens when we go our own way. But, most importantly, He was showing us through all these stories and rules, that we cannot do it ourselves. We cannot live the Way He want's us to live - in a way that is BEST for us - by doing things our own way. Without Him.

And so, He sent Jesus.

Jesus came not only to show us the Way, but to BE the Way for us. Don't worry - even His disciples who were with Him all the time for like 3 years were confused by this. They asked, "Lord, we do not know where you are going. How can we know the way?" to which He answered, "I am the Way, the Truth, and the Life." (John 14:5-6)

Oh...

???

Uhhhhmmm... I'm not sure about you, but this doesn't clear things up for me!

The answer lies in what Jesus said time and time and time again.

Follow me.

FOLLOW me.

Follow ME.

He didn't say COPY me. He said FOLLOW me.

He knew He was about to die, but in that death He made a way for His Spirit to actually dwell in us. When we listen to (and obey!) that Spirit, we are following Him.

Following is an action. We can't just check off the, "I believe in Jesus," box and call it good. He calls us to action. It means paying attention and actually moving... WITH Him.

I find when I stop following Him (and go my own way,) I end up in a spot. A BAD spot. And then I freak out and cry, "God, why did you abandon me?!" Of course, He never abandons us. We stop following Him and we get lost. But He WANTS us to find Him and follow Him, and He assures us that we WILL find Him when we seek for Him with all our heart. (Jeremiah 29:11-13)

Okay, so... this all SOUNDS really easy. Just follow.

But it's not. Especially at first.

You see, at first we're not used to listening. We're not used to hearing His voice. His voice is soft. And gentle. And quiet. We're used to listening to the voice of the world, which is loud, and harsh, and obnoxious, like a "SUNDAY, SUNDAY, SUNDAY!!!" commercial for some monster truck rally!

But, when we start listening to His voice, we become more familiar with it. The more we follow Him, the more we see how His ways ARE better than our ways, (even though they may not seem so at first!) and we learn to trust Him more. We learn to listen more. We become the sheep who know His voice and do not listen to the voice of a stranger. (John 10:4-5) This means using our will. We CHOOSE to follow Him.

So, how do we start following Him? How do we start listening to His voice? He speaks to each of us differently... in the way that WE need to hear. For me, it's a gentle nudge, or a strong prompting. And I know it's Him, (and not the voice of a stranger,) when there is PEACE in the decision. If there's no peace, then it's not from Him, because the fruit of the Spirit is Love, Joy, PEACE... If I get the prompting to turn left, and there's peace in that decision, (even if I have no idea where "left" is going to lead me!) and if it's not in contradiction to His Word, then I know it's from Him. But, that's just one of the ways He speaks to ME.

How does He speak to you? Ask Him. He WANTS you to hear Him. More than that, He wants you to LISTEN, which means we must first be silent. And then, in the silence, a still, small voice saying, "Follow me..."

May we all follow Him.

In Jesus' name.

Amen.

~ ~ ~ ~ ~ ~ ~ ~ ~ ~ ~ ~ ~

SCRIPTURES

John 14:5-6 ~ Thomas said to him, "Lord, we do not know where you are going. How can we know the way?" Jesus said to him, "I am the way, and the truth, and the life. No one comes to the Father except through me."

Jeremiah 29:11-13 ~ For I know the plans I have for you, declares the Lord, plans for welfare and not for evil, to give you a future and a hope. Then you will call upon me and come and pray to me, and I will hear you. You will seek me and find me, when you seek me with all your heart.

John 10:4-5 ~ When he has brought out all his own, he goes on ahead of them, and his sheep follow him because they know his voice. But they will never follow a stranger; in fact, they will run away from him because they do not recognize a stranger's voice.

John 21:21-22 ~ When Peter saw him, he said to Jesus, "Lord, what about this man?" Jesus said to him, "If it is my will that he remain until I come, what is that to you? You follow me!"

HOW THEN SHALL WE PRAY?

PRAY WITHOUT CEASING

*J*esus answers this question in Matthew 6:9-13 by giving us what we now refer to as, "The Lord's Prayer." He said, "Pray like this: Our Father Who is in heaven, hallowed be Your name. Your kingdom come, Your will be done on earth as it is in heaven. Give us this day our daily bread, and forgive us our debts as we forgive our debtors. And lead us not into temptation, but deliver us from evil. For Thine is the kingdom and the power and the glory, now and forever. Amen."

I've read books on prayer and have heard the Lord's prayer broken down into 4 parts, easily remembered by the word ACTS:

A - Adoration

C - Confession

T - Thankfulness

S - Supplication

I have used this format in my journaling, only because it helps organize my thoughts. However, sometimes things like this may make it seem like if we follow this outline and pray in this way, we will be doing it "right" and God will then hear our prayers. I'm totally a recipe girl and I love any step-by-step process for doing things the "right" way, (especially when it comes to pleasing God!) but this feels more like "religion" than "relationship" to me... and religion kinda scares me. (Matthew 6:5)

Okay... relationships do too, a lot of the time!

But, I don't think God wants our relationship with Him to be scary... or prayer to be done out of fear or obligation. I know I don't want MY kids to have to think about some formula for how to speak to me when they come to me with an issue or request. Obviously I'd like them to be respectful, but that comes from a place of love, not some rule-based list of do's and don'ts they must refer to before approaching me.

To me prayer is a conversation with someone I love. In my heart and mind, I'm talking to my Beloved... my Dad... my Mom... my Best Friend ... not some distant deity who has little time or regard for me or my problems. (Psalm 8:4) Yes, He is the Creator of the Universe, (never to be forgotten – hence the "Hallowed be Your name" part!) but He is also the One Who loves me (ME – not just some random human who is a part of the human race and therefore MUST be loved by default... but ME specifically,) and He so desperately wants to spend the rest of eternity with me that He gave up everything to make sure that happened. (John 3:16-17) I'm talking to the Maker and Lover of my soul. (Psalm 139:13)

And that's Who He is for YOU as well.

Therefore, we don't have anything to hide... because we CAN'T have anything to hide. (Psalm 139:7-8) We don't have to come groveling before Him like some filthy worm hoping to gain an audience with Him. He is always right here with us and is ALWAYS listening. Even in our sin. (2 Chronicles 7:14) He doesn't JOIN us in our sin, but He sees every bit of it... and He STILL loves us. (Romans 5:8) And even though He already knows everything, including everything we want and need, (Matthew 6:7-8) He still WANTS to hear from us. In fact, I believe He oftentimes WAITS to hear from us before doing anything, because He wants us to be a part of the miracle that is this life.

More often than not we only start talking to God by using what Anne Lamott (one of my favorite writers,) refers to as her most powerful prayer. It goes something like this:

"Dear God. Help help help help help help help!!"

While this is how I first started talking to God, now I really, really, REALLY want my prayers to be my first line of defense... not my last resort.

I have a very dear friend who always strikes me by how he prays. His prayers usually go something like this, "Yeah God, good morning... it's me again. Thanks for this morning. The sunrise was really great. Thanks for letting me see another one. Thanks for my friends here. Please help them out with what they're dealing with. Please give 'em what they need and not what they don't. Help us all get through this day, as I know you will, but please let it end well with not too much crap in between. Thanks for how you love us and for all you do for us. In Christ's name I pray. Amen."

I love his reverent familiarity and no-nonsense communication.

The Word tells us to "Pray without ceasing." (1 Thessalonians 5:17) For me this practice, (and it IS something I practice, because I'm FAR from perfect at it!!) looks something like this...

I wake up and thank God for my husband. "Abba, thank you for the gift of this most amazing man that I love SOOO much!"

I open my blinds and see the sunrise, the pink clouds, hear the birds, see the robins hopping around the grass searching for unsuspecting earthworms and I say, "Thank you, Abba, for another glorious day. Please make me aware of Your Spirit today. Please give me wisdom and discernment, and eyes to see and ears to hear."

As I start my day at work I say, "Lord, please help me accomplish all the tasks that YOU set before me – not all the ones *I* (or others!) think need to be done, but the ones YOU want me to accomplish. Thank You for allowing me to be a part of Your plan for today."

When I'm driving through town and I'm following someone who's actually going the speed limit, or I'm stopped at another red light, I say, "Thank you, Lord for this opportunity to practice patience." *deep sigh*

When I see a beaten down and weary soul on a bike or pushing a cart with a bulging backpack and several bags of cans to be recycled I say, "Lord, please be with them today. Please wrap Yourself around them and make Your loving presence known to them. Please keep them safe and warm, and guide them according to Your will."

When I see deep sorrow and pain and shattered dreams in someone's eyes and I ask them how they're doing and they say, "Fine," not wanting to vomit their soul into my lap, I pray, (with them if they'll let me, or silently if they're uncomfortable with that,) "Dear Abba, I lift this hurting heart up to You for Your gentle healing. Please reveal Yourself in a profound way in their life right now and relieve some of the suffering... even if it is self-inflicted."

When I'm in the middle of something and suddenly someone comes to mind who I know is going through a challenging, frightening or overwhelming time right now, I pray, "Father, please be with them right now. Please help them and encourage them. Please let them feel Your presence and know that You are with them, so they have nothing to fear. (Romans 8:31) Please remind them of Your love for them. In Jesus' name. Amen."

When I'm being torn down and judged and ridiculed by someone, I pray, "Sweet Jesus, please heal them. You know the hurt in their heart that is causing them to feel this insecurity and I pray that you would please help them stop hurting, and stop hurting others."

As I'm sipping my delicious tea or coffee, I say, "Oh, dear God... thank you, thank you, thank you!"

All day, every day there are countless opportunities to pray, which is why we can "pray without ceasing" – literally.

So, Lord, I pray that You would deepen our relationship with You and help us to feel more comfortable with just talking with You throughout our day. Thank You for bringing us back into relationship with You through Jesus... and it's in His name I pray. Amen.

~ ~ ~ ~ ~ ~ ~ ~ ~ ~ ~ ~ ~

. . .

SCRIPTURES

Matthew 6:9-13 ~ Pray like this: Our Father Who is in heaven, hallowed be Your name. Your kingdom come, Your will be done on earth as it is in heaven. Give us this day our daily bread, and forgive us our debts as we forgive our debtors. And lead us not into temptation, but deliver us from evil. For Thine is the kingdom and the power and the glory, now and forever. Amen. (ESV)

Matthew 6:5 ~ When you pray, don't be like the hypocrites who love to pray publicly on street corners and in the synagogues where everyone can see them. I tell you the truth, that is all the reward they will ever get. (NLT)

Matthew 6:7-8 ~ And when you pray, do not keep on babbling like pagans, for they think they will be heard because of their many words. Do not be like them, for your Father knows what you need before you ask him. (NIV)

Psalm 8:4 ~ What is man that You think of him, and a son of man that You are concerned about him? (NASB)

John 3:16-17 ~ For this is the way God loved the world: He gave his one and only Son, so that everyone who believes in him will not perish but have eternal life. For God did not send his Son into the world to condemn the world, but that the world should be saved through him. (NET)

Psalm 139:13 ~ You made all the delicate, inner parts of my body and knit me together in my mother's womb. (NLT)

Psalm 139:7-8 ~ Where shall I go from your Spirit? Or where shall I flee from your presence? If I ascend to heaven, you are there! If I make my bed in Sheol, you are there! (ESV)

2 Chronicles 7:14 ~ if my people, who are called by my name, will humble themselves and pray and seek my face and turn

from their wicked ways, then I will hear from heaven, and I will forgive their sin and will heal their land. (NIV)

Romans 5:8 ~ But God demonstrates his own love for us, in that while we were still sinners, Christ died for us. (NET)

Romans 8:31 ~ What then shall we say to these things? If God is for us, who can be against us? (NKJV)

1 Thessalonians 5:17 ~ pray without ceasing

FOR GOD SO LOVED...

CAN YOU FINISH THAT SENTENCE?

ey Scripture ~ *For God so loved the world, that he gave his only begotten Son, that whosoever believeth in him should not perish, but have everlasting life.* ~ *John 3:16 (KJV)*

This is probably THE most famous verse in the Bible. Even "non-believers" can quote this! Which is why I think we're really in trouble here... this has become SO familiar, that we don't really GET what it's saying. It's like we just hear, "blah blah blah... more Bible talk... blah blah blah..."

Let's take a little test...

Replace "the world" in that quote, with the word, "me"...

Can you do it?

Can you say, "For God so loved ME that He gave His only begotten son..."

The REAL question is, do you BELIEVE it?

The thing that truly breaks my heart - and I'm certain it breaks God's heart as well - is how many people, (even "believers"!) don't really "believe" God truly loves them.

I grew up kinda seeing God as this grumpy grampa, always scowling at me, watching me like a hawk, with one eyebrow raised, just waiting for me to do something wrong so he could whack me with his cane!

I "knew" God "loved" me, but I kinda felt like someday I was gonna get to heaven and He'd be like, "Oh. It's you. *deep sigh and eye roll* Well... I see here you checked the box that says you "believe in Jesus," so I guess I HAVE to let you in. Come on... hurry up, before I change my mind!"

It took a long time of wrestling with God, (and I mean SERI-OUSLY WRESTLING with Him!) before it started to sink in that He really DOES love me. And, what TOTALLY blew my mind, is when I started to realize that he actually LIKES me, too.

We think we have to fix ourselves first... get our act together... clean up our thoughts and our lives and our language before God could POSSIBLY love us. I heard one dear friend, (who is a homeless alcoholic, and who REALLY loves Jesus,) say that God wants no part of him, because he's just a loser.

That's what he's been told by people for way too long. And I'm sure, like me, you've been told similar things... things that basically say, "You're not good enough!"

But story after story after story - both in the Old and the New Testament - say otherwise.

The Message translation of Deuteronomy 7:7-10 says, (about God choosing the nation of Israel,) "God wasn't attracted to you and didn't choose you because you were big and important—the fact is, there was almost nothing to you. He did it out of sheer love... Know this: God, your God, is God indeed, a God you can depend upon. He keeps his covenant of loyal love with those who love him and observe his commandments for a thousand generations."

And in the New Testament Paul tells us in Romans 5:6-8 that God's love for us has nothing to do with us. He says, "Christ... didn't, and doesn't, wait for us to get ready. He presented himself for this sacrificial death when we were far too weak and rebellious to do anything to get ourselves ready. And even if we hadn't been so weak, we wouldn't have known what to do anyway. We can understand someone dying for a person worth dying for, and we can understand how someone good and noble could inspire us to selfless sacrifice. But God put his love on the line for us by offering his Son in sacrificial death while we were of no use whatever to him."

That is how God loves us.

So much, that He sent Jesus to DIE so He could spend forever with us.

With me.

With YOU.

He loves us like that right now.

Just as we are.

Right now.

And THAT, my friend, is the good news that we ALL need to hear! Whether for the first time, or the hundredth time... we all need to hear - and BELIEVE - how much we are loved.

In Jesus' name.

Amen.

BAD TO THE BONE

BUT THERE'S GOOD NEWS!

*I*n my experience, most people really don't think they need Jesus. I think the (mostly subconscious) thought process goes something like this...

"Yeah, I'm sure I'll go to heaven when I die. After all, I'm a pretty good person. I don't cheat on my taxes (much) or my wife. (Though thank God that woman in that movie last night doesn't live next door! Whew!) I work hard, (at least harder than the other schmucks at the office!) and I almost never lie. (Except when my wife asks if that dress makes her look fat - but, then... that's for my own self preservation!) I'm a law abiding citizen, (everyone goes 5-7 mph over the speed limit!) and I love my country. (When the guy I voted for is in office.) Yep. When I die I'm sure I'll go to heaven because, all in all I'm really a pretty good person, and God knows that. In any event, I'm WAAAAY better than THAT guy!"

We think this way because we COMPLETELY don't understand who God is. (Honestly, I'm totally okay with not understanding everything about God... I mean, if I could understand God with my tiny little brain, then He's not very much of a God - and I need a MUCH bigger God than that! *laughing*)

And that's just the thing. We think God is just like us.

Only a little smarter.

And a little bigger.

And a little wiser.

And a little better.

But that is completely wrong.

Frank Wedekind, a German playwright in the late 1800's and early 1900's, is credited with saying, "God made man in his own image, and man returned the favour."

But God is NOT like us.

We are made in His image, but that doesn't mean God is like us. That's kind of like saying if you've seen a photograph of Yosemite, or the Grand Canyon or Crater Lake then you've experienced it. But anyone who has ever BEEN to one of these places knows full well that no photograph could ever capture the awesome majesty of these places. We are made in His image, but, even in all our "goodness" we are a far cry from being as good as God. Even the best person we can think of falls short of His perfection.

I once heard it explained like this...

Let's say you write the name of the best person you can think of (besides Jesus) on one card and the name of the worst (most evil) person you can think of on another. The best person's card you take to the top of the highest building, while you place the evil person's card on the sidewalk below.

Let's say the best person is that much "higher" than the evil person.

But God's goodness is past the furthest star in our universe... He's THAT much "higher" than even the best person we can think of. And again, that's a lot for my little brain to comprehend.

God tells us in Isaiah (55:8-9) "For my thoughts are not your thoughts, neither are your ways my ways,"declares the Lord. "As the heavens are higher than the earth, so are my ways higher than your ways and my thoughts than your thoughts."

And, being perfect, our sin cannot come anywhere near Him. We literally would burn up in His presence, like a piece of lint in a fire.

But again, we think, we're not THAT bad. We're basically pretty good.

J.D. Greear (in his AWESOME book, Not God Enough,) used the analogy of getting a blood transfusion and finding out 1% of the blood you received was infected with HIV. Are you any less infected because it's only 1%???

The same is true with sin. There is no percentage... you've either got it, or you don't. And trust me... we've ALL got it. It's in our blood. We are all bad to the bone! And there is nothing WE can do to improve our condition.

And THAT'S why what Jesus did is called the Good News!

God KNEW we would never be able to cleanse ourselves... no matter what we do or how hard we try. We are infected and the only thing that can truly cleanse us is new blood.

His blood.

And, THAT'S the Good News! He's already given it for us.

For all of us.

For free.

All we need to do is accept it.

And THEN the awesome adventure begins!

In Him!

BOTH AND

NOT EITHER OR

*G*rowing up I used to pray, "Lord, please help me to be a positive example." This especially became my prayer when I became a mother! But, as I traveled through life I veered off the "path of righteousness" and down some pretty dark and desolate paths before finally turning back to The Truth.

Coming back to Jesus was NOT easy. Don't get me wrong... HE welcomed me back immediately, and there was ALWAYS peace in my prayers and time with Him. But, there were those who were still on the "other" paths and did not want me to leave them, and sadly, there were some on the "right" path who saw the baggage I carried with me as an opportunity to add to my shame. I even had one "friend" continuously tell me what a bad mother I was, saying, "You always wanted to be a positive example, but instead you're just a horrible warning!" Oftentimes I felt like I brought all my sins to the foot of the cross, and others would pick them up and beat me with them.

It took me years, but I finally learned to distance myself from hurtful "friends" and take my sins directly to Jesus in prayer.

While always Truthful, He is never "brutally" honest - He is loving and kind in His teaching... difficult though it may be.

Recently, I said something I knew I shouldn't have said, (completely ignoring that still small voice (1 Kings 19:11-12) of the Holy Spirit!) and just charged on ahead with what I had to say. Afterwards, of course, I felt absolutely terrible, and started listening to that old familiar recording in my head, telling me what a complete failure I was. As is the usual pattern, I then started reliving ALL my past failures, until I was in tears.

Finally, I started to pray. (I say "finally" because there are times when I must have life literally drive me to my knees before I remember what I should do when I'm there! *sigh*)

I first asked for forgiveness, not only for what I'd said, but mostly for disobeying the guidance of the Holy Spirit.

Immediately, I felt a peace flood my heart, like a warm hug from Jesus Himself.

"I'm so sorry," I said to Him. "I HATE failing."

"I know you do..." I felt Jesus reply to my heart, "...that's called pride." I immediately felt ashamed, but He continued softly, "You're learning, my child. You only "fail" if you don't try again."

"I always want to be a positive example," I cried, "but just like my friend said, I've just been a horrible warning."

"It's actually both and." Jesus answered. "You're both a positive example AND a horrible warning."

This didn't make me feel any better, so Jesus continued.

"Being "both and" is not a bad thing. Abraham was both and. Moses was both and. David was both and... the only person who has never failed, is Me... People don't need to see that you're perfect... they need to see HOW and WHAT you do WHEN you fail. Do you blame other people or circumstances and rail against the world? (Proverbs 14:1) Or do you humble yourself, ask for forgiveness, and try again? It's good to keep trying, but be gentle with yourself in the process. When a toddler is learning to walk, you don't scold them when they fall and tell them what a failure they are. You help them up, brush them off, and encourage them to try again. (John 8:10-11) Treat yourself like the child of God that you are." (1 John 3:1)

He sat with me quietly as I let His words sink into my heart.

"Failure is actually a small success. It's a good thing, when you allow it to teach you." He finally said softly. "You learn what DOESN'T work, so you're that much closer to finding what DOES." It felt like He gently kissed me on the forehead as I finally drifted off to sleep.

I know I'm not alone in this struggle, so I'm sharing this with you... hopefully you can come to peace with BOTH the positive example AND the horrible warning that you are as well.

In Jesus' name.

Amen.

~ ~ ~ ~ ~ ~ ~ ~ ~ ~ ~ ~ ~

SCRIPTURES

1 Kings 19:11-12 ~ And he said, Go forth, and stand upon the mount before the Lord. And, behold, the Lord passed by, and a great and strong wind rent the mountains, and brake in pieces the rocks before the Lord; but the Lord was not in the

wind: and after the wind an earthquake; but the Lord was not in the earthquake: And after the earthquake a fire; but the Lord was not in the fire: and after the fire a still small voice. (KJV)

Proverbs 14:1 ~ A wise woman builds her home, but a foolish woman tears it down with her own hands. (NLT)

John 8:10-11 ~ Jesus straightened up and asked her, "Woman, where are they? Has no one condemned you?" "No one, sir," she said. "Then neither do I condemn you," Jesus declared. "Go now and leave your life of sin." (NIV)

1 John 3:1 ~ See what kind of love the Father has given to us, that we should be called children of God; and so we are...

CHOOSE LIFE

NOT A PERMANENT SOLUTION TO TEMPORARY PROBLEMS

*S*ometimes life can get so dark, it feels like giving up and ending it is the only answer. But giving up on life is a permanent solution to a temporary problem, (it just transfers your pain to those who love you!) and it's exactly what the enemy wants you to do. That's what "satan" means - enemy.

You are a beautiful light in this world, uniquely created by God, (in His very image!) and satan wants more than anything to put your light out.

You may have peace in the idea of an easy solution, (we all want things to be easier!) but true peace only comes from God, so you'll never have peace about suicide. Because suicide is NEVER God's will, He'll never give you peace about it.

All this you're going through is just the crap of life. It's how we learn and grow. Remember, "crap" is fertilizer that enriches the soil, so have faith in the fertilizer! Yes, it's difficult, and yes it stinks, but you can learn from this. You can grow from this. You are strong.

But.

You.

Have.

To.

Choose.

Life.

And listen to those who truly love you!

God truly loves you. Read His love letter to you. The more you have His Word in your heart and mind, the less room there is for the lies of the enemy.

Satan doesn't love you. He hates what a light you are in this world, so he fills your head with darkness, trying to put your light out. This is why we're instructed to put on the full armor of God - which includes the helmet of salvation to protect our minds!

The Bible says, "Resist the devil and he will flee from you." It doesn't say you have to fight Him. After you put on the full armor of God, you stand firm! The battle is spiritual. Whenever you have negative thoughts you know they're from the enemy, so do not listen to the voice of a stranger. Tell him to shut the hell up (literally!) because Jesus already defeated him and his time is short.

Read it OUT LOUD from the Word - and the devil WILL leave you. He has to! He is the father of lies and he hates the Truth. Oh, he'll come back, (sometimes really soon!) just to see if you meant what you said, but you just tell him again... and again... and again, 1000 times if you must.

It's a discipline... but that's why we're called disciples.

I'm not just talking. I've had many, many, many days, weeks, months, and even years of being right where you are... wishing I could just quit breathing... wishing it could all be over. I'm speaking from experience.

The Bible says, "He will keep you in perfect peace when your mind is fixed on Him, because you trust Him." So, we keep bringing our thoughts back to Him... remaining in Him. Keep focusing on the positive. Keep on keeping on! It never ends, but it does get easier. It's hard at first, just like any exercise, but the more you do it the stronger you get. Nobody else can control your mind... satan can't and God loves you too much to do so. He gave us free will, so we get to choose.

But, don't think you must go through this alone.

You are never alone.

God will not allow more than you can handle, so turn to Him for help. Pray for His Holy Spirit to comfort you. He has good plans for you, and He will be found by you when you seek Him with all your heart.

So, turn to Him.

And, choose life.

(If you are thinking of harming yourself, please call 800-273-8255 - Suicide Prevention Hotline, 800-525-5683 to speak with a pastor, or 911 for immediate assistance.)

https://suicidepreventionlifeline.org/talk-to-someone-now/

https://ww2.klove.com/ministry/pastors

~ ~ ~ ~ ~ ~ ~ ~ ~ ~ ~ ~

. . .

SCRIPTURES

Genesis 1:27 ~ So God created man in his own image, in the image of God he created him; male and female he created them. (ESV)

Matthew 5:16 ~ Let your light so shine before men, that they may see your good works, and glorify your Father which is in heaven. (KJV)

Ephesians 6:12 ~ For our battle is not against flesh and blood, but against the rulers, against the authorities, against the world powers of this darkness, against the spiritual forces of evil in the heavens.

Philippians 4:8 ~ Finally, brethren, whatever is true, whatever is honorable, whatever is right, whatever is pure, whatever is lovely, whatever is of good repute, if there is any excellence and if anything worthy of praise, dwell on these things. (NASB)

John 15:4 ~ Remain in me, as I also remain in you. No branch can bear fruit by itself; it must remain in the vine. Neither can you bear fruit unless you remain in me. (NIV)

James 4:7 ~ Submit yourselves therefore to God. Resist the devil, and he will flee from you. (KJV)

Ephesians 6:10-18 ~ Finally, be strong in the Lord and in his mighty power. Put on the full armor of God, so that you can take your stand against the devil's schemes. For our struggle is not against flesh and blood, but against the rulers, against the authorities, against the powers of this dark world and against the spiritual forces of evil in the heavenly realms. Therefore put on the full armor of God, so that when the day of evil comes, you may be able to stand your ground, and after you have done everything, to stand. Stand firm then, with the belt of truth buckled around your waist, with the breastplate of righteousness in place, and with your feet fitted with the readiness that comes from the gospel of peace. In addition to all this, take up the shield of faith, with which you can extinguish all the flaming arrows of the evil one. Take the helmet of salvation and the sword of the Spirit, which is the word of God. And pray in the Spirit on all occasions with all kinds of prayers and requests. With this in mind, be alert and always keep on praying for all the Lord's people. (NIV)

Revelation 12:12 ~ Therefore, rejoice, O heavens and you who dwell in them! But woe to you, O earth and sea, for the devil has come down to you in great wrath, because he knows that his time is short!" (ESV)

Deuteronomy 30:15-20 ~ I call heaven and earth as witnesses today against you, that I have set before you life and death, blessing and cursing; therefore choose life, that both you and your descendants may live; that you may love the Lord your God, that you may obey His voice, and that you may cling to Him, for He is your life and the length of your days; (NKJV)

Colossians 1:13 ~ He delivered us from the power of darkness and transferred us to the kingdom of the Son he loves (NET Bible)

1 Corinthians 9:24 ~ Do you not know that in a race all the runners compete, but [only] one receives the prize? So run [your race] that you may lay hold [of the prize] and make it yours. (AMPC)

John 10:5 ~ They won't follow a stranger; they will run from him because they don't know his voice. (NLT)

John 8:44 ~ He (the devil) was a murderer from the beginning, not holding to the truth, for there is no truth in him. When he lies, he speaks his native language, for he is a liar and the father of lies. (NIV)

John 14:6 ~ Jesus said to him, "I am the way, and the truth, and the life. No one comes to the Father except through me." (ESV)

1 Corinthians 10:13 ~ No trial has overtaken you that is not faced by others. And God is faithful: He will not let you be tried beyond what you are able to bear, but with the trial will also provide a way out so that you may be able to endure it. (NET Bible)

John 14:16 ~ And I will pray to the Father, and he shall give you another Comforter, that he may abide with you for ever (KJV)

Psalm 139:7-8 ~ I can never escape from your Spirit! I can never get away from your presence! If I go up to heaven, you are there; if I go down to the grave, you are there (NLT)

Jeremiah 29:11-13 ~ For I know the thoughts and plans that I have for you, says the Lord, thoughts and plans for welfare and peace and not for evil, to give you hope in your final outcome. Then you will call upon Me, and you will come and pray to Me, and I will hear and heed you. Then you will seek Me, inquire for, and require Me [as a vital necessity] and find Me when you search for Me with all your heart. (AMPC)

Luke 4:13 ~ When the devil had finished every temptation, he left Him until an opportune time. (NASB)

DESIGNED BY DIVINITY

BE WHO HE CREATED YOU TO BE

*A*t the very core of our being... the very root of each and every one of us - is the amazing, glorious truth that we need God. There is an ache in our heart - a desperate desire in our soul that can only be filled by our Divine Beloved. And that truth drives us to our knees.

But, if we do not surrender to this glorious truth... if we do not bend our will to succumb to this embrace, then one of two lies shoot forth...

The first lie is that we DON'T need God. We are just fine. We are good people. We do the right things, go to work, pay our taxes - we even claim to be Christians. But, we don't really NEED God. We are too smart for that.

The other swing of the pendulum says that we aren't good enough for God. With all that we've said and done... as much pain and suffering as we've been through and caused... there is no way God would ever want anything to do with us. We're way beyond hope.

But Solomon - with all his wisdom... with all his wealth and fame and wives and glory... with all that he had at the end of his life, he realized that it was all a "chasing after the wind"... that all he really needed, was God.

And David... and adulterous murderer - was a man after God's own heart.

Moses... also a murderer who may have had a speech impediment and whose anger issues not only led him to murder, but also caused him to throw down the tablets of the 10 commandments that had been inscribed by the finger of God, and ALSO caused him to strike the rock to bring forth water for the Israelites, (instead of just speaking to it as the Lord commended,) resulting in his not being allowed to cross over into the promised land... he was called "the most humble man on earth" and a man of God whom the Lord spoke with face-to-face.

If Solomon the Great needed God, then no matter how great and wise we think we are, we need Him too.

And if God could love and forgive David and Moses of their sins against Him, then He will forgive our sins as well.

Both of these thoughts - that we're good enough or NOT good enough - have a root of pride. And pride is what drove satan from the throne room of God.

It is in humility that we see ourselves as we truly are. Glorious creations designed by Divinity - frail and fragile without His indwelling Spirit.

We are nothing without Him.

Only with Him can we be all he created us to be.

So we pray...

Abba, thank You for Your Holy Spirit. Please strengthen us with Your strength. Give us Your wisdom, Your grace, Your mercy, Your forgiveness, and Your great love - for ourselves and for others. Please help us to be the beautiful people You created us to be.

In Jesus' name.

Amen.

INDEPENDENCE

WHAT ARE WE SLAVES TO?

*J*ohn 8:36 says, "So, if the Son makes you free, you will be free indeed!"

But, what does it mean to be independent?

The dictionary tells us it is to be "free from outside control." Oftentimes we relate this to slavery – which is exactly what this particular passage is referencing...

But what is this really talking about? What are we slaves to??

Slaves to our sin?

Slaves to our selfish desires?

Slaves to our personal comfort?

Slaves to our habits?

Slaves to each other?

We are slaves to anything that controls us.

To be truly "independent" is to be "free from outside control"

– and this is exactly what Jesus does... He sets us free from outside control. Free from the control of external forces.

The ironic thing is we give up being slaves to sin when we give up our lives to Christ. We willingly become a "slave" (or a bond-servant) to Jesus... so we've basically just traded one form of "slavery" to external control, for another one of internal control!

However... in John 15:15 we see the true heart of the Lord revealed. We see how He really wants our relationship with Him to be. He tells us, "No longer do I call you slaves... but I have called you friends."

Wow. That just melts my heart! *laughing* What joy!

Jesus doesn't want us to "serve" Him out of some religious place of prideful obedience. He wants us to be His friend. Someone who loves Him and would do anything for Him out of that place of deep relationship... deep companionship... deep devotion.

Jesus wants me to give up my independence to be in dependence on Him.

Ahhhh.... may this be my heart.

Always.

In Him.

Amen.

NEVER ALONE

NO MATTER WHAT YOU FEEL

I heard someone say once that their life goal was, "to go to heaven and take everyone in the world with them." I love that! Maybe because it's *similar* to my own life goal, which is basically, "to have a deeper relationship with Jesus and to do everything I can to encourage others to do so as well!" To me, that's what it's all about. Not just "getting to heaven" but having a deeper relationship with Him.

In my article on the Trinity, I summarized "my relationship with Him" by breaking it down into His 3 aspects, which I'll share again here:

FATHER ~ Growing up, I didn't really have a dad. I never met my real father, (he's passed,) and every other "dad" that came along made many promises and kept very few. And so "Father God" became my "Abba" – my "Daddy" – my "Father who art in heaven." He's always kept His promises. He's always there when I need Him. And, no matter what, He loves me. He loves me so much that He sent Jesus to die for me, (John 3:16) so I could be with Him forever.

SPIRIT ~ When I was young my mom and I did NOT get along, so the Holy Spirit became my "Mother" of sorts. (Jesus told us God is Spirit (John 4:24) and we (male and female) were made in His image, (Genesis 5:1-2) so I have no issues with seeing the Holy Spirit as a "Mother" figure.) The Spirit is the one who counsels me, who comforts me when my heart is broken, and whose raised eyebrow I can feel from across the room when I'm about to do something I know I'm not supposed to do. The Spirit pulls no punches in telling me when I've messed up, but also forgives me immediately when I admit it, and then helps me make it right and/or not do it again.

SON ~ And then, there's Jesus. Growing up He was always kind of just an acquaintance of mine. I knew Him, and He was cool to hang out with sometimes at church, but outside of church we didn't really talk much. Until I got older. Until I got hurt. Actually, it wasn't until I decided I was DONE being hurt. Then I realized that I was supposed to be HIS bride. He wasn't just there to hang out with at church, He wanted me by His side. As His...

I share this because it wasn't until I really understood, (though, I still don't think I "really" understand!) how much He loves me, and how His love for me doesn't change, (no matter what I do or don't do!) that I started to REST in this understanding. I started to believe that He was Who He said He was... and He was that FOR ME.

This really sank in for me several years ago when I was traveling for work. It was the middle of the night and I couldn't sleep because I was all alone in a hotel room, in a not-too-great part of town... far from home with no friends or family nearby. There was no one I could call at that hour. There was no one that could come over and hang out or talk with me.

I was all alone.

And I felt it.

But then I thought, "Wait a minute... what about God?! Are You there, God?? Are you HERE???"

And then suddenly I felt His presence, and I heard Him whisper into my heart, "Yes, My child. I am ALWAYS here. I am always with you... even when you can't hear me or feel me or sense my presence... I am here. I am with you always. I am. Even to the end of the age. You are NEVER alone."

That was truly a life-altering realization for me.

So, let me ask you... do YOU realize this?? Do YOU realize that God is only a prayer away??

Always?

KNOW this...

In the middle of the night, when you can't sleep... He's there.

When you're working on a project and you're overwhelmed by all you have to do... He's there.

When you feel like you're drifting and don't know what direction you need to take... He's there.

When you're faced with seemingly insurmountable odds and you feel like there's no way out... He's there.

You just need to turn to Him.

You don't need to earn His love.

Just like the thief on the cross, all you need to do is turn to Him. (Luke 23:42-43)

He is there.

Always.

To the end of the age. (Matthew 28:20)

You are NEVER alone.

AMEN!

~ ~ ~ ~ ~ ~ ~ ~ ~ ~ ~ ~

SCRIPTURES

John 3:16 ~ For God so loved the world that he gave his one and only Son, that whoever believes in him shall not perish but have eternal life. (NIV)

John 4:24 ~ For God is Spirit, so those who worship him must worship in spirit and in truth. (NLT)

Genesis 5:1-2 ~ He created them male and female; when they were created, he blessed them and named them "humankind. (NET)

Luke 23:42-43 ~ Then he said, "Jesus, remember me when you come into your kingdom." Jesus answered him, "Truly I tell you, today you will be with me in paradise." (NIV)

Matthew 28:20 ~ I am with you always, to the end of the age. (ESV)

SHAME ON YOU

NO NO NO NO NO!

The Bible is FULL of "shameful" situations where we (humans) fail over and over and over again, from Adam and Eve, to things like Abraham and Sarah, Moses's anger issues, (and murder!) David's adultery, (and murder!) and on and on and on, all they way through to Jesus' disciples... and beyond!

The first story of shame we have in the Bible is of course, Adam and Eve. After eating the forbidden fruit, they realized they were naked and were ashamed. (If we're truly honest about our sin, it always makes us feel "naked" (vulnerable) and ashamed before God.) They make a lame attempt to hide their nakedness from each other, (by sewing fig leaves together,) then they make another lame attempt to hide from God, and when He asks them what they've done they start a blame game about why they sinned.

In the end, God protects them... not only from the possibility of eating from the Tree of Life and living forever in this now shameful "sinful" state, but He is also the one who adequately covers them.

This is the first actual death in the Bible - perhaps the first "sacrificial lamb" here... God showing love, grace and mercy as He covers the very first sinners with that very first sacrifice.

We see this pattern time and time and time again throughout the Bible. Over and over and over again, we read how God protects and loves and shows grace and mercy to shameful humans who have done shameful things. But, for now, lets jump all the way to the New Testament, and look at two of the most famous stories of shame we see there. First, let's remember Peter's shame.

Early in the evening (just after the "last supper") Jesus makes the announcement that ALL His disciples would abandon Him. Peter jumps up and adamantly assures Jesus that he would NEVER do such a thing, to which Jesus calmly responds that yes, Peter WILL deny Him - 3 times in fact, this very night, before the rooster crows...

A short while later, in defense of Jesus, Peter cuts off the ear of the servant of the High Priest in the garden, for which he is sharply rebuked by Jesus. It quickly becomes clear that this is not going to end well for any of them, so all of Jesus' disciples, including Peter, run for their lives, afraid that they too will be arrested with Jesus.

Peter however, follows Jesus at a distance, and hangs out in the courtyard where he can kind of eavesdrop and keep tabs on what's happening to Him. It is here that Peter is confronted and accused of being one of Jesus' followers, which he intensely denies. The 3rd time he is questioned, he becomes absolutely furious, starts calling down curses on himself, and again, denies it vehemently.

And then... a rooster crows.

Can you imagine that??? My heart jumps into my throat every time I read this passage.

Peter must have frozen when he heard that rooster.... his heart jumping into his throat as well, as he suddenly remembers Jesus' words from just a few short hours before. Time stands still as he turns towards where Jesus is being interrogated...

... and Jesus turns and looks directly at him.

Oh.

My.

Goodness.

This nearly destroys Peter, and he runs out of the courtyard weeping bitterly.

I imagine the next few days were excruciating for Peter, as I've experienced first hand shame's relentless torment, and how it will cruelly abuse us for as long as it possibly can.

Finally, Peter decides he's going fishing - back to something familiar. The other disciples go as well, (remember, they ALL abandoned Jesus in the garden, just as He predicted, so they're all fighting their own shame,) but it turns out to be another long, cold night of failure, and they catch nothing.

Suddenly, at dawn, a familiar Voice from the shore calls out to them... just to see how they're doing. Upon hearing they've caught nothing all night, the Voice directs them to throw their nets on the right side of the boat, (that sounds VERY familiar!) and when they do so, they catch so many fish they're unable to haul in the nets! Yes! They've experienced this before, and John says to Peter, "It is the Lord!"

That is all the confirmation Peter seems to need! He immediately dives off the boat and swims to shore, desperate for that familiar Voice standing on the beach to silence the vicious voice of shame in his head.

When Peter, drenched to the bone and bone weary from the battle, climbs out of the water and stumbles through the sand to Jesus, he is shown love, grace, and mercy.

AND he's fed a nice hot breakfast!

Now, on to Judas.

While we obviously don't know exactly WHY Judas chose to betray Jesus, (some believe it was an attempt to force His hand and pressure Him into becoming their "King"?) what's important is not only that he DID betray Him, but maybe more importantly, what Judas did (and did not do) afterwards...

From what we read in scripture, Judas' kiss in the garden was the last time he interacted with Jesus, with Jesus' last words to him being, "Judas, are you betraying the Son of Man with a kiss?" and "Do what you came for, friend."

Perhaps this actually pierces Judas' heart... perhaps this causes Judas to begin to feel the depth of what he's done. He later learns that Jesus is condemned to die, and in a desperate attempt to undo his dirty deed, he tries to return the payment he received from the Pharisees back to them. They, of course, are completely unsympathetic towards him, and refuse to take the money back. So, he throws the silver coins into the temple, runs off...

...and hangs himself.

Judas never returned to Jesus.

Let us always remember WHY Jesus came. To FINISH what was started by Adam and Eve in the garden. (And perpetuated by each and every one of us.) He came to show love, grace, and mercy to anyone who would come to Him. To anyone who would return to Him. It is only His voice that can silence the ruthless voice of shame that echoes relentlessly in our hearts and minds.

Hear this truth my friend... what Jesus did is FAR greater than anything you've ever done.

Therefore, when you come to Him, He covers you, just like God did with the first sacrifice in the garden. Jesus was the final, the ultimate sacrifice, and through that sacrifice, He covers you with His goodness. You are clothed with His righteousness.

He showers you with His love.

With His grace.

With His mercy.

And in that shower, all your "bad" is washed away by all His "good"... Jesus washes you completely clean.

So, now there is no no no no NO MORE shame on you!

In Jesus' name!

Amen!

~ ~ ~ ~ ~ ~ ~ ~ ~ ~ ~ ~

<u>SCRIPTURES</u>

Genesis 3 ~ Adam & Eve's shame

Genesis 16 ~ Abraham & Sarah's shame

Numbers 20:11 ~ Then Moses raised his hand [in anger] and with his rod he struck the rock twice [instead of speaking to the rock as the Lord had commanded]. And the water poured out abundantly, and the congregation and their livestock drank [fresh water]. (AMP)

Exodus 2:11-12 ~ One day, when Moses had grown up, he went out to his people and looked on their burdens, and he saw an Egyptian beating a Hebrew, one of his people. He looked this way and that, and seeing no one, he struck down the Egyptian and hid him in the sand. (ESV)

2 Samuel 11:1-13 ~ David's adultery

2 Samuel 11:14-17 ~ David murders Uriah

Matthew 26:31-35 ~ Then Jesus said to them, "You will all fall away because of me this night. For it is written, 'I will strike the shepherd, and the sheep of the flock will be scattered.' But after I am raised up, I will go before you to Galilee." Peter answered him, "Though they all fall away because of you, I will never fall away." Jesus said to him, "Truly, I tell you, this very night, before the rooster crows, you will deny me three times." Peter said to him, "Even if I must die with you, I will not deny you!" And all the disciples said the same. (ESV)

John 18:10-11 ~ Then Simon Peter drew a sword and slashed off the right ear of Malchus, the high priest's slave. But Jesus said to Peter, "Put your sword back into its sheath. Shall I not drink from the cup of suffering the Father has given me?" (NLT)

Mark 14:50 ~ Then all his disciples deserted him and ran away. (NLT)

Luke 22:60-62 ~ Peter replied, "Man, I don't know what you're talking about!" Just as he was speaking, the rooster crowed. The Lord turned and looked straight at Peter. Then Peter remembered the word the Lord had spoken to him: "Before the rooster crows today, you will disown me three times." And he went outside and wept bitterly. (NIV)

John 21 ~ Peter goes fishing & gets breakfast

Luke 22:48 ~ But Jesus said to him, "Judas, are you betraying the Son of Man with a kiss?" (NKJV)

Matthew 26:48-50 ~ Now the betrayer had arranged a signal with them: "The one I kiss is the man; arrest him." Going at once to Jesus, Judas said, "Greetings, Rabbi!" and kissed him. Jesus replied, "Do what you came for, friend." (NIV)

Matthew 27:3-5 ~ Then when Judas, who had betrayed Him, saw that He had been condemned, he felt remorse and returned the thirty pieces of silver to the chief priests and elders, saying, "I have sinned by betraying innocent blood." But they said, "What is that to us? You shall see to it yourself!" And he threw the pieces of silver into the temple sanctuary and left; and he went away and hanged himself. (NASB)

John 19:30 ~ When Jesus had received the sour wine, he said, "It is finished," and he bowed his head and gave up his spirit. (ESV)

Isaiah 61:10 ~ I delight greatly in the Lord; my soul rejoices in my God. For he has clothed me with garments of salvation and arrayed me in a robe of his righteousness, as a bridegroom adorns his head like a priest, and as a bride adorns herself with her jewels.

Hebrews 10:10-12 ~ Our sins are washed away and we are made clean because Christ gave His own body as a gift to God.

He did this once for all time. All Jewish religious leaders stand every day killing animals and giving gifts on the altar. They give the same gifts over and over again. These gifts cannot take away sins. But Christ gave Himself once for sins and that is good forever. After that He sat down at the right side of God. (NLV)

TRINITY

MY OWN FAMILY

*D*on't worry... I am not going to try to explain, or define, or try to comprehend, or try to get YOU to comprehend, the Trinity.

The Father.

The Son.

The Holy Spirit.

It's way, way, WAY too big for me.

I totally agree with what He says in Isaiah 55:9... as the heavens are higher than the earth, so are His ways higher than my ways and His thoughts than my thoughts. And honestly, I'm okay with that. I want God to be God and me to be me. I WANT God to be bigger than anything I can explain or define or try to comprehend!

But... there's still a part of me that wants to know Him more. Better. Deeper. Allowing Him to reveal Himself to me in different ways is part of how I'm allowed to experience Him more. Better. Deeper.

And so, I will share with you how He has revealed Himself to me, and maybe, in some small way, this may help you allow Him to reveal Himself to you uniquely as well.

(This is very childlike and simple, but Jesus said in Luke 18:16 that the Kingdom of Heaven belongs to such as these! *smile*)

FATHER

Growing up, I didn't really have a dad. I never met my real father, (he's passed,) and every other "dad" that came along made many promises and kept very few. And so "Father God" became my "Abba" – my "Daddy" – my "Father who art in heaven." He's always kept His promises. He's always there when I need Him. And, no matter what, He loves me. He loves me so much that He sent Jesus to die for me, (John 3:16) so I could be with Him forever.

SPIRIT

My mom and I did NOT get along when I was young, so the Holy Spirit became my "Mother" of sorts. (Jesus told us God is Spirit (John 4:24) and we (male and female) were made in His image, (Genesis 5:1-2) so I have NO issues with seeing the Holy Spirit as a "Mother" figure.) The Spirit is the one who counsels me, who comforts me when my heart is broken, and whose raised eyebrow I can feel from across the room when I'm about to do something I know I'm not supposed to do. The Spirit pulls no punches in telling me when I've messed up, but also forgives me immediately when I admit it, and then helps me make it right and/or not do it again.

SON

And then, there's Jesus.

Growing up He was always kind of just an acquaintance of mine. I knew Him, and He was cool to hang out with sometimes at church, but outside of church we didn't really talk much. Until I got older. Until I got hurt. Actually, it wasn't until I decided I was DONE being hurt. Then I realized that I was supposed to be HIS bride. He wasn't just there to hang out with at church, He wanted me by His side. As His. And when I finally surrendered to Him being my Beloved and me being His bride, that is when He showed me how much He loves me, by bringing the most amazing man into my life and loving me through him more completely than I've ever experienced, or even dreamed possible.

So... there's these three. The Father. The Son. And the Holy Spirit.

Different, yet... all God – right? How?

Again, I don't really get it... but when I was praying more about it, I got an example of how 3 things can be very different, and yet be the same thing.

Water.

In it's liquid form, it's kind of like Abba. The mighty oceans, the roaring rivers, the gentle rain.

When it's a gas, like steam or clouds, it's like the Holy Spirit... always present and yet a bit elusive.

Jesus became flesh. He's more solid, like ice and snow.

3 very different ways of experiencing water... and yet, they're all water. So, I personally don't think it really matters HOW we experience God, or Jesus, or the Holy Spirit. I think what matters is that we DO experience Him. That we open our hearts enough to allow Him to reveal Himself to us in whatever way He wants to, whether its clouds or rain or snow.

. . .

~ ~ ~ ~ ~ ~ ~ ~ ~ ~ ~ ~ ~

SCRIPTURES

Isaiah 55:9 ~ For as the heavens are higher than the earth, so are my ways higher than your ways and my thoughts than your thoughts. (ESV)

Luke 18:16 ~ But Jesus called them [the parents] to Him, saying, Allow the little children to come to Me, and do not hinder them, for to such [as these] belongs the kingdom of God. (AMPC)

John 3:16 ~ For God so loved the world that he gave his one and only Son, that whoever believes in him shall not perish but have eternal life. (NIV)

John 4:24 ~ For God is Spirit, so those who worship him must worship in spirit and in truth. (NLT)

Genesis 5:1-2 ~ When God created humankind, he made them in the likeness of God. He created them male and female; when they were created, he blessed them and named them "humankind." (NET)

TRY TRY TRY AGAIN

ASHAMED??

*K*ey Scriptures ~ *On one occasion, while the crowd was pressing in on him to hear the word of God, he was standing by the lake of Gennesaret, and he saw two boats by the lake, but the fishermen had gone out of them and were washing their nets. Getting into one of the boats, which was Simon's, he asked him to put out a little from the land. And he sat down and taught the people from the boat. And when he had finished speaking, he said to Simon, "Put out into the deep and let down your nets for a catch." And Simon answered, "Master, we toiled all night and took nothing! But at your word I will let down the nets." And when they had done this, they enclosed a large number of fish, and their nets were breaking. They signaled to their partners in the other boat to come and help them. And they came and filled both the boats, so that they began to sink. But when Simon Peter saw it, he fell down at Jesus' knees, saying, "Depart from me, for I am a sinful man, O Lord." For he and all who were with him were astonished at the catch of fish that they had taken, and so also were James and John, sons of Zebedee, who were partners with Simon. And Jesus said to Simon, "Do not be afraid; from now on you will be* *catching men." And when they had brought their boats to land, they left everything and followed him. ~ Luke 5:1-11*

... but whoever denies me before men, I also will deny before my Father who is in heaven. ~ Matthew 10:33

In the story from Luke chapter 5, Jesus has just blessed these weary fishermen with an abundance of fish - clearly a supernatural sign, as they'd been fishing all night and had caught nothing! When Peter realizes WHO it is he's in the boat with, he says to Him, "Depart from me, for I am a sinful man, O Lord."

Oh.... how I can relate to Peter! *deep sigh*

So often in my life, I am ashamed to call myself a Christian.

Jesus said, "...whoever denies me before men, I also will deny before my Father who is in heaven," and I don't want THAT! It's not that I'm ashamed of Jesus at all... I want EVERYONE to know WHO He is and what He's done!

I'm ashamed... of myself. Of my thoughts and my actions... my words and my deeds.

Sometimes I don't want ANYONE to know I'm a Christian, only because I don't want them to think Jesus, (or even His followers!) are anything like ME!

It's times like these when I want to fall on my knees like Peter and cry, "Depart from me, oh Lord. I'm soooo sinful!"

But if I read on in this same passage, Jesus says to Peter, "Fear not..." and goes on to tell him of His plans for his life... that Jesus will make him a fisher of men.

Jesus KNEW who Peter was.

He KNEW what he'd done.

And He KNEW what he was GOING to do.

Peter would DENY Him. (More than once!)

And yet Jesus says, "Fear not…"

Why???

I believe it's because Jesus KNEW Peter's HEART.

Just like He knows mine.

Just like He knows yours.

He knows WE will deny Him, (more than once… probably daily!) in our behavior, actions, words or deeds.

And, this is why He taught us to pray DAILY, "forgive us our sins…"

The key is, He knew Peter would run out of the courtyard weeping after denying Him.

THAT is a repentant heart.

And THAT is what He wants from us.

More than us wearing a cross or having a fish symbol or a "Jesus Saves" bumper sticker on our car or us asking every person we meet if they have a personal relationship with Jesus Christ. He wants a broken and contrite heart. He wants a heart that WANTS to obey. In 1 Samuel we are told that God wants obedience more than anything else. He wants our heart.

HE wants a personal relationship with US.

Even if we have to repent over and over and over again.

And THAT is how we show people Who Jesus really is.

Not that WE'RE perfect, but that HE is... and that He is loving and gracious and forgiving, and that if He can forgive someone as messed up as ME, then He can and will forgive someone as messed up as them as well.

Does this mean we can just do whatever we want because we KNOW we'll be forgiven? Of course not. (Romans 6) It means when we slip up, the grace of Jesus is there to catch us and set us back on our feet so we can try again.

And again.

And again.

And again.

And again.

Thank God!

In Jesus' name.

Amen.

YOUR INMOST BEING

YOU ARE WONDERFULLY MADE

*K**ey Scripture* ~ *For you created my inmost being;
you knit me together in my mother's womb.* ~
Psalm 139:13 (NIV)

*"The sculpture is already complete within the marble block,
before I start my work. It is already there, I just have to chisel
away the superfluous material."* ~ *Michelangelo*

When you were created, you were perfect. Who you are - your
inmost being - is perfect. You were designed by Divinity.

And then you came into this fallen world...

The hostile ruler of this world hates God and anything God
makes, so he does everything in his power to destroy it. And
so, from the moment we're born, this world starts throwing
junk (superfluous material) onto us... like clay just being
thrown at the pot on the artist's wheel, adding more and more
and more until we're this lumpy bumpy mass of hardened lies.

Lies about who we truly are.

Lies that say we're too fat or too skinny or too tall or too short or too young or too old or too weak or too blah blah blah... fill in the blank. They're all lies that want us to believe we're not loved. That we CAN'T be loved. Because we're not lovable.

Lies, lies, LIES!!!

But, there's good news.

The truth is in there...

Who you TRULY are, is in there.

You may not have ever known who you TRULY are.

But, God knows.

And it's His plan to show you.

However... just like Michelangelo chiseling away at the sculpture to reveal the glorious sculpture that is hidden inside, so God must do the same to us.

And so, He allows us to be in situations that grate on us...

Situations that rub us the wrong way.

Situations that make us feel like we're in a rock grinder... spinning around and around and around, tumbling over and over and over in sloppy slimy sandy gritty muck and mire.

I know.

I've been there.

And while I NEVER would have chosen it, and I wouldn't wish it on my worst enemy... I wouldn't change it for anything in the world.

Because it chiseled away those rough edges of my personality.

It softened my sharp tongue.

It smoothed gritty nature.

It revealed the true me that was under all that stuff that WASN'T me.

It revealed the true me that is loved by God.

I know He's not finished with me yet... just like He's not finished with you yet, either.

He doesn't make junk. You were wonderfully made. (Psalm 139:14)

He made you because He loves you. And, all the lies and other garbage that gets thrown at you and on you from this world can never change that... can never change who you TRULY are.

He sees the beautiful you beneath all the lies.

And He wants YOU to see that beautiful person, too.

Abba, please give us eyes to see ourselves as you see us. Please remove the scales from our eyes so we can see clearly. Help us to be the people you created us to be, and to radiate Your Spirit more and more each day, as you whittle and chip and grind and chisel away the lies from our lives. And please, give us the strength and perseverance to endure it, because we need it! In Jesus' name we pray. Amen.

ABOUT THE AUTHOR

Dart is the gifted and inspired creator of the website, aBranchOnTheVine.com. The site is a brilliant faith-based blog designed to help us know the uncomplicated truth about Jesus.

A Christian for most of her life who has overcome obstacles including mental, emotional, and physical traumas, Dart knows the Jesus she follows and is passionate about communicating His goodness to the world.

By day, Dart is the Manager of Learning & Development for a global outdoor recreation company. She spends her evenings serving the homeless in her community alongside the love of her life, John, who is the Director of Low Barrier Service for a local non-profit, long-term rehabilitation organization, homeless shelter and navigation center.

Read more from Dart at aBranchOnTheVine.com, or send her an email at Dart@aBranchOnTheVine.com

f